Let's Pray

30 DAYS OF PRAYER

SHAVONDA G. MCCALEB

Shavonda G. McCaleb

Printed in the United States of America

All Rights Reserved.

No part of this book may be reproduced or transmitted in any form or by any means, electronic or mechanical, including photocopying and recording, or by any information storage and retrieval system, without the permission in writing from the publisher and the author. Thank you for the support of the author's rights.

First Edition: March 2018

Unless otherwise noted Scriptures are taken from the *Holy Bible*, King James Version (KJV), New International Version (NIV), The Message Bible (MSG), English Standard Version (ESV)

Cover Design by SDAP Marketing

Copyright © 2018 by Shavonda G. McCaleb, LLC

ISBN-13: 978-0-9991308-5-8

For more information contact Publisher:

Leading Through Living Community

6790 W. Broad Street

Douglasville, GA 30134

ALSO BY SHAVONDA G. MCCALEB

He Meant It for My Good

Daily Inspirations

If It Can Be Done, We Can Do It

Warning Signs

DEDICATION

This book is dedicated to my son, Jonathan McCaleb. You know from personal experience that PRAYER WORKS! I praise God that even during your own battle with an unexpected illness, even as a young man, you kept the faith and believed God through His WORD and PRAYER!

Keep Praying, Baby!

-Love Mom

To those of you who have cried and prayed, and prayed and cried, in search for answers to the matters of your heart; be encouraged knowing that Prayer STILL Works!

SPECIAL THANKS

Special thanks to my Spiritual Life Coach Mario C. Brown. Your wisdom, insight, tenacity, strength, compassion, dedication, and love for God's people exemplify what it means to be a genuine and authentic leader after God's own heart! Thank you for not giving up on me and PUSHING me when I wanted to quit and throw in the towel. Thank you for challenging me to keep PRESSING pass my pain and frustration. Thank you for allowing me to be naked and vulnerable in my weakest moments. I am BETTER, BOLDER, WISER, and WHOLE because of your spiritual guidance and LOYAL friendship. Thank You!

- Shavonda G. McCaleb

Shavonda G. McCaleb

CONTENTS

	Dedication	iv
	Special Thanks	v
	Foreword	Ix
	Preface	xi
	Lord Hear My Prayer	1
Day 1	Prayer of Thanksgiving	5
Day 2	Prayer of Repentance	9
Day 3	Prayer of Salvation	13
Day 4	Prayer for A Praying Spirit	17
Day 5	Prayer for Guidance & Direction	21
Day 6	Prayer for Wisdom	25
Day 7	Prayer for Knowledge	29
Day 8	Prayer for Understanding	33
Day 9	Prayer for Peace of Mind	37
Day 10	Prayer for Unspeakable Joy	41
Day 11	Prayer for Courage & Boldness	45
Day 12	Prayer for Unity	49
Day 13	Prayer for Patience	53
Day 14	Prayer to Rid Insecurities	57
Day 15	Prayer to Release Guilt	61
Day 16	Prayer to Dance to the Rhythm of God	65

Day 17	Prayer for Self-Control	69
Day 18	Prayer to Eliminate Weakness	73
Day 19	Prayer for Clarity at A Dead End	77
Day 20	Prayer to Trust God Beyond the Broken Pieces	81
Day 21	Prayer for Personal Growth	85
Day 22	Prayer to Discharge Depression	89
Day 23	Prayer for Perseverance – How Much Longer?	93
Day 24	Prayer of Exaltation	97
Day 25	Prayer of Newness	101
Day 26	Prayer to Desire Him More	105
Day 27	Prayer of Learning (School is in Session)	109
Day 28	Prayer for the Chase – Don't Get Tired	113
Day 29	Prayer for A Drink (Let's Have A Drink)	117
Day 30	Prayer of Breaking News	121
	WE BELIEVE	125

FOREWORD

Prayer Works!

God hears the big and small, gigantic and tiny, utterly outrageous and inconsequential prayers. He hears the hopeful and hopeless, happy and sad, inspiring and desperate prayers. And He answers them all.

Not in our time or in our way, but in His time and in His Holy way. According to His will and what is best for not only our good but the good of those who love Him and are called to His purpose. Romans 8:28

But why is it some prayers seem to be heard before others? Why it is some people's prayers seem to have more power than others? What qualifies people as prayer warriors?

A life of prayer. Simple and yet not so simple.

Developing and implementing a strong prayer life requires one to pray consistently, often, without fail, and sincerely. Daily prayer focused on behavior that is pleasing to the Lord is a wonderful start to a beautiful prayer life.

But a prayer life requires discipline and structure. It requires commitment and sincerity. It requires one to pray even when the desire is not there, when the fire and excitement have waned, when there are bills to pay, deadlines to meet, expectations to exceed, and people to care for.

Prayer disciplines the mind, softens the heart, strengthens the spirit, and steadies the emotions. Prayer expands creativity, enhances mental agility, deepens compassion and opens one's life to all the wonder and the wow that God's goodness and grace has to offer.

Let's Pray: 30 Days of Prayer is the jump start to your spiritual rejuvenation and renewal. Shavonda McCaleb has created this beautiful guide to begin and continue a strong prayer life. Her sincere love and hope for your life shines through every word; it is a beacon of all the good things to come. Follow it to a deeper understanding of and relationship with The Holy Spirit.

May God bless and keep you my brothers and sisters in Christ.

Lynita Mitchell Blackwell, Esq., CPA, CCLC

First Lady, Saint Paul AME Church Smithfield

Birmingham, Alabama, USA

PREFACE

Let's Pray was written with you in mind. This book is intended to draw you closer to God through the power of prayer. It has been said that if we as human beings do something consecutively for 21 days, it becomes a habit. My prayer is just that for you – that prayer will become a habit in your life.

What exactly is prayer? Prayer is communication between you and the Father - it is a dialog and not a monolog. It's essential that when we commune with the Father that we take time to 'listen' and 'wait' for Him to speak. I'm sure that you have many unanswered questions that you have brought to God's attention and wondered why you haven't received an answer. May I ask you a question? Have you taken the time out to wait for Him to speak or did you say what you had to say and ended the conversation without pausing in His presence for an answer?

You see, prayer is essential for the believer, just like water is a necessity for the human body. To learn and grow in any relationship, communication is critical. One thing about prayer: you can be open, honest, and naked with the Father and not worry that what you shared will be uncovered by others.

Over the next 30 days, I would encourage you to position yourself to communicate with the Father properly. Don't just pray; allow some time to wait for His presence. My prayer for you is that during the next 30 days, the matters of your heart will be settled and your mind at ease, knowing that you have placed those matters in secure hands. Remember, before God starts working on your request, He first starts working on your heart. Don't rush the process, ENJOY the 30-day prayer journey that you are about to embark upon and hold on to Psalms 138:8: "The Lord will perfect that which concerns [you]". He cares, He knows, and He's looking forward to spending quality time with you. Enjoy the Journey and Journey Well.

-Shavonda G. McCaleb

LET'S PRAY

LORD, HEAR MY PRAYER

When asked to write this section of Shavonda's body of work, I was tasked with establishing the tone for the reader to proceed with confidence and assurance, knowing God will hear and answer our prayers. While I was honored to be asked to participate in this project, I was also very contemplative as to what the Holy Spirit wanted to convey. As a man of prayer, I have developed a reliance on prayer as a guiding source to obtain the fellowship, direction, peace, and assurance from God the Father in times of insurmountable circumstances. I understand many people have a tough time with the matter of prayer due to the invisibility of God. The original scripture speaks to this by letting us know that God is Spirit. Therefore, as much as God is in the invisible realm, His spirit is authentic and present in the earthly kingdom.

To know the purest and most simple definition of prayer is to see the power of prayer. Prayer is nothing more than our confession that we need help. Our helplessness indicates to God our need for His divine intervention and provision. I have the utmost confidence that as you embrace this definition of prayer, you will find the missing link in your spiritual life.

The Psalmist wrote, "I am praying to you because I know you will answer, O God. Bend down and listen as I pray." (Psalm 17:6) This psalm expresses the speaker's confidence in God's ability and willingness to hear his prayer. The language exhibits a portrait of God bending down, as one would to a little child, to speak with and says, "Listen as I pray." I encourage you to know today God's ear is not too heavy that it cannot hear, nor is His arm too short that it cannot save. You are only a pray away from help, miracles, and divine intervention.

LET'S PRAY...

Father in the Name Jesus,

We thank you for lending us your ear and your heart. God, you told us in your word men ought to always pray. We ask that every person who would read this book would experience the divine power of God. Father, make them one with prayer. Drench them with grace to believe that you hear them when they pray. Father, remove fear, doubt, and unbelief from the mind, heart, and spirit of those who will take this 30-day journey. Release miracles, answers, and directions over the next 30 days. Let them feel your presence as they partner with the prayers in this book. Reveal that which has been hidden, speak to the dead places, and stir up gifts, talents and abilities. Show your people a pathway to empowered living by making prayer an intricate part of their daily life.

Father, as your people pray, let their enemies become their footstool and prepare a table for them in the presence of their enemies. Reveal your perfect will, and establish yourself as their God. Dismantle the plan of the enemies of their prosperity. Defend them against the assault of every adversary. We plead the precious blood of Jesus that was shed on Calvary for the remission of our sins. Give divine protection. Save families, restore marriages and broken family relationships. Break the back of poverty. Release abundance through obedience. Change hearts and minds in the name of Jesus. Give victory where there has been defeat. Give healing where there is sickness and the spirit of infirmity. Grant peace in chaos. Release the power of the Almighty God in every life so that each person will yield to the Lordship of Jesus Christ.

We ask this in the name of Jesus,

Amen.

Pastor Mario C. Brown | www.mariocbrown.org

Prayer is Our Confession that we need help

DAY 1

PRAYER OF THANKSGIVING

Father, today I pause before a fully loaded schedule to offer you a sincere and humble prayer of Thanksgiving! I know that if it were not for your Goodness, Grace, and Mercy; I would not be where I am today in life. No, not everything has been smooth and yes, at times I wanted to give up and throw in the towel. But you kept me in the midst of it all, and I want to say THANK YOU!

I am ashamed to admit that many days I started and ended without saying thank you. Many times you have opened doors and blocked the hand of the enemy and I did not say thank you. There were moments in my life when you made a way out of no way and I did not say thank you.

Father, I know that I cannot make up for the missed opportunities and moments in my life, but I want to stop right now and offer you a prayer of thanksgiving.

Thank you for this precious moment you have granted me to be in your presence. Thank you for keeping me, even when I did not want to be kept. Thank you for sending your angels who excel in strength to cover me when I was weak and lost. Thank you, Father, for loving me with everlasting love.

Thank you for being who you are in my life. It is because of you that I breathe the breath of fresh air day after day. It is because of you that I am in my right mind. It is because of you that I am appropriately positioned in the posture of prayer, offering you true and sincere thanksgiving on today.

Nevertheless, most importantly, THANK YOU for saving my soul and thank you for being the real difference maker in my life.

In Jesus' name, Amen!

SCRIPTURE READING

I Thessalonians 5:16-18 says, "Be joyful always; pray continually; give thanks in all circumstances, for this is God's will for you in Christ Jesus."

Psalm 136:1 says, "Give thanks to the Lord, for He is good. His love endures forever."

Hebrews 12:28 says, "Therefore, since we are receiving a kingdom that cannot be shaken, let us be thankful, and so worship God acceptably with reverence and awe."

LET'S PRAY: 30 DAYS OF PRAYER

MY PERSONAL PRAYER

Shavonda G. McCaleb

Thank you for keeping me

DAY 2

PRAYER OF REPENTANCE

Father, I do not know where to start. I tried and failed again. I have let You down on so many levels, and I do not feel worthy to ask for Your forgiveness. Every time I try to do what is right, I find myself doing what is wrong. Even though I know what I am doing is against Your will, I continue to do it.

So today, I come to You with my hands lifted as a sign of surrender. I surrender this flesh and stubborn will to You. I yield my thoughts that continue to tell me that wrong is right and right is wrong. I surrender to You my all at this very moment!

I pray this prayer of REPENTANCE with an open heart for a change. Not an outward change; rather, Father CHANGE ME from the inside out! Create in me a clean heart, and renew a right spirit within me.

I repent from a sincere place, and I ask You for total forgiveness. I regret all the wrong that I have done in my life. I repent of the wrongful deeds I have done to others. I repent for taking people's kindness for weakness. I regret not overlooking my brother's and sister's faults and shortcomings. I repent of the precious time I have wasted that You have given me. I repent of things I have done in my past and present.

Father, I repent of my sinful ways today and turn my back from sin. Order my steps, leading and guiding me in the right direction You have mapped out for my life.

In Jesus' name, Amen!

SCRIPTURE READING

Acts 13:38 declares, "Therefore, my brothers, I want you to know that through Jesus the forgiveness of sins is proclaimed to you."

Acts 3:19 declares, "Repent, therefore, and turn back, that your sins may be blotted out."

Acts 26:20 declares, "I preached that they should repent and turn to God and prove their repentance by their deeds."

LET'S PRAY: 30 DAYS OF PRAYER

My Personal Prayer

Shavonda G. McCaleb

Father CHANGE ME from the inside out

DAY 3

PRAYER OF SALVATION

Father, I know that real SALVATION is more than an ordinary confession from my lips to Your ears. It is a matter of the heart, and GRACE and FAITH encompass it.

Father God, you said in Romans 10:13, "Whosoever shall call upon the name of the Lord shall be saved." Therefore, today I call upon You to come into my heart and my life and SAVE ME!

With my heart, I BELIEVE, and with my mouth, I CONFESS that JESUS IS LORD and I BELIEVE that You, God, raised Jesus from the dead.

This day, I choose to turn from my sinful ways. I decide to follow You. I want to live according to the Word of God. I wish to be a living testimony of what true salvation looks like.

Thank You, Father, for saving my sin-sick soul. Thank You for loving me enough to provide me an opportunity to be that guiding light in a dark place for others to find their way. Thank You for saving me for such a time as this and not allowing me to remain in my sin.

I am SAVED, in Jesus' name, Amen!

SCRIPTURE READING

Romans 10:9-10 says, "If you confess with your mouth, 'Jesus is Lord,' and believe in your heart that God raised him from the dead, you will be saved. For it is with your heart that you believe and is justified, and it is with your mouth that you confess and are saved."

Ephesians 2:8-9 says, "For by grace you have been saved through faith. And this is not your own doing; it is the gift of God, not a result of works, so that no one may boast."

Romans 10:13 says, "Whosoever shall call upon the name of the Lord shall be saved."

LET'S PRAY: 30 DAYS OF PRAYER

My Personal Prayer

I want to live according to the Word of God

DAY 4

PRAYER FOR A PRAYING SPIRIT

Father, thank You for the privilege of prayer!

Today, I bow humbly at Your throne asking You to endow me with a praying spirit. A praying spirit that prays according to the Spirit's leading. A praying spirit that goes beyond mere words, but praying the word of God, allowing the Holy Spirit to make intercession on my behalf. Lord, when I pray, give me what to say. I say yes to Your will and yes to Your way. I surrender this flesh to You.

As I go throughout this day, help me to be sensitive to the Holy Spirit. Help me to keep my ear pressed to Your lips while You are speaking so that I do not miss You. Help me to wrap everything that concerns me and others in prayer.

As I pray today, Father *"let the words of my mouth and the meditation of my heart be acceptable in Your sight," (Psalms 19:14)*. You are my rock and my redeemer, and I don't want to do anything or say anything that doesn't please You.

As I petition the throne for myself and others, I pray that You send Your angels, mighty in strength, to cover me from the crown of my head to the souls of my feet.

In Jesus' name, Amen!

SCRIPTURE READING

Ephesians 6:16-18 says, "In all circumstances take up the shield of faith, with which you can extinguish all the flaming darts of the evil one; and take the helmet of salvation, and the sword of the Spirit, which is the word of God, praying at all times in the Spirit, with all prayer and supplication. To that end, keep alert with all perseverance, making supplication for all the saints."

Romans 8:26 says, "Likewise the Spirit helps us in our weakness. For we do not know what to pray for as we ought, but the Spirit himself intercedes for us with groanings too deep for words."

My Personal Prayer

Shavonda G. McCaleb

Keep my ear pressed to Your lips while You are speaking

Day 5

PRAYER FOR GUIDANCE & DIRECTION

Father, thank You for another opportunity to come before You. As my Heavenly Father, I know that there are no limits or boundaries between us because You are more than able to assist me.

So I come to You today asking You to provide me with Your guidance and direction regarding the matters of my heart. I know doing things on my own has not turned out for my best. Therefore, if You are behind the steering wheel of my life, I'm convinced You will guide me in the right direction – the one You have ordained for my journey.

I tried it my way, and nothing seemed to work, so, I'm placing the matters of my heart into Your more than capable and steady hands. Where You lead me Father, I will follow. I know with confidence that where You guide, You will provide.

So, I thank You for the new journey that I am about to embark upon. Thank You for leading and guiding me in the right direction You, the one ordained by You and set clearly before me. Thank You that the matters of my heart are now resolved because I am on the right path and I will stay on track.

In Jesus' name, Amen and so be it!

SCRIPTURE READING

Psalm 25:4-5 says, "Show me your ways, Lord, teach me your paths. Guide me in your truth and teach me, for you are God my Savior, and my hope is in you all day long."

Psalm 61:1-2 says, "Hear my cry, O God; listen to my prayer. From the ends of the earth, I call to you, I call as my heart grows faint; lead me to the rock that is higher than I."

Psalm 16:7-8 says, "I will praise the Lord, who counsels me; even at night my heart instructs me. I keep my eyes always on the Lord. With him at my right hand, I will not be shaken."

LET'S PRAY: 30 DAYS OF PRAYER

My Personal Prayer

Shavonda G. McCaleb

You will guide me in the right direction

Day 6

PRAYER FOR WISDOM

Father, thank You for the love I'm feeling right now. Thank You for being the One I can come to for wisdom concerning my life and decisions that will affect the lives of many.

Father, I pray now that You will give me the wisdom to handle the situations that I am dealing with. Give me the understanding to make sound decisions without being affected by my emotions. Give me the knowledge to calm a stormy sea. Give me the wisdom to lead and guide my family in a healthy way. Give me the wisdom to win souls for the Kingdom. Give me the wisdom I need to be a constant light for a dark world.

Father, give me the wisdom to make sound and accurate decisions as it relates to my ministry, business, education, career, marriage, children, family, relationship, and friendships. Break old patterns that I have grown accustomed and comfortable with, and give me the wisdom to change. Give me the wisdom to change my behavior, attitude, and tone when I am dealing with Your people. Give me the wisdom that I need to execute the plans You have set before me correctly.

Father, I believe with Your help that I will begin to make sound decisions with the wisdom that You have granted me on this day. So, I say thank You for hearing my prayer for wisdom, for Your word says in James 1:5, *"If anyone lacks wisdom, you should ask God, who gives generously to all without finding fault, and it will be given to you."*

Father, I'm standing on your word believing that you will give me the wisdom I need to make it through the situations and circumstances that I am facing. I have asked, I believe, and therefore Wisdom shall be mine on today!

In Jesus' name, Amen!

SCRIPTURE READING

Proverbs 2:6 says, "For the Lord gives wisdom; from his mouth come knowledge and understanding.

James 3:17 says, "But the wisdom that comes from heaven is first of all pure; then peace-loving, considerate, submissive, full of mercy and good fruit, impartial and sincere."

Proverbs 16:16 says, "How much better to get wisdom than gold, to get insight rather than silver!"

My Personal Prayer

Give me the wisdom to make sound and accurate decisions

DAY 7

PRAYER FOR KNOWLEDGE

Jesus, you are the perfect example of wisdom, knowledge, and understanding. I pray today that You pour on me your instruction from above. I've tried attaining knowledge through books, from the world, and in the streets; they have failed me.

Today, I seek Your face for real knowledge and understanding. The kind of knowledge that will not cause me to question my integrity when I put it into action. I know that the fear of the Lord is the beginning of wisdom, and from Your mouth comes understanding and knowledge. So, grant me this day a humbled spirit and a teachable heart to apply the knowledge that I will gain on today.

Father, I pray for a more excellent knowledge of You as I travel on this road called Life. I pray now that You will continue to endow me with more of your understanding of the word, grace, mercy; and how to handle Your people so I may be a pure reflection of You and not an embarrassment to the Kingdom!

Teach me how to handle the knowledge that You have given me this day – everything that I do and everyone whom I encounter. Help me to resemble You and Your word. Keep me humble with the knowledge that I have attained.

In Jesus' name, Amen!

SCRIPTURE READING

Proverbs 18:15 says, "An intelligent heart acquires knowledge, and the ear of the wise seeks knowledge."

Proverbs 1:7 says, "The fear of the Lord is the beginning of knowledge; fools despise wisdom and instructions."

Hosea 4:6-7 says, "My people are destroyed for lack of knowledge; because you have rejected knowledge, I reject you from being a priest to me. And since you have forgotten the law of your God, I also will forget your children. The more they increased, the more they sinned against me; I will change their glory into shame."

My Personal Prayer

I pray for a more excellent knowledge of You

DAY 8

PRAYER FOR UNDERSTANDING

Father, it's me again! Today is another one of those days where I feel overwhelmed, lost, confused and stuck! I can't seem to make sense of everything that is going on at this intersection of my life. Things are not going according to plan. My life looks as if it is on a downward spiral and things are spinning out of control.

I pray now that You would touch my mind and erase everything that I've come up with as it relates to this situation. I ask that You would pour into me Your understanding of the situation and how I should handle it. Give me the understanding to see things as You know them. Open up my mind to receive the lesson that is being taught through this condition I am in.

Father, take me in Your arms and give me rest from this. Hold me in Your arms and comfort my mind and heart from these confusing times.

Father, help me to obtain a clear understanding of what is happening in my life and what You have assigned me to do. Help me not to miss You and please help me not to abort this process that I am in – GIVE ME A GODLY UNDERSTANDING!

In Jesus' name, Amen!

SCRIPTURE READING

Jeremiah 33:3 says, "Call to me and I will answer you and tell you great and unsearchable things you do not know."

Proverbs 14:29 says, "Whoever is patient has great understanding, but one who is quick-tempered displays folly."

Romans 10:13 says, "Whosoever shall call upon the name of the Lord shall be saved."

LET'S PRAY: 30 DAYS OF PRAYER

My Personal Prayer

Shavonda G. McCaleb

Pour into me Your understanding

DAY 9

PRAYER FOR A PEACE OF MIND

Father God, thank You for the privilege of prayer. Thank You for granting me access to a day that wasn't promised to me. A day that I did not deserve to see, and I am grateful to be in the land of the living.

Today I come to You because I am in need of PEACE. I'm asking that You would give me peace of mind, in body, soul, and spirit. My soul is unrested, and I am unable to make clear decisions because I do not have any peace in my mind or heart right now. I am losing sleep and rest is nowhere to be found. Help me, Father!

Father, please bestow upon me the kind of peace that Your word talks about that surpasses all human understanding *(Philippians 4:7)*. Please remove any and everything in my life that is causing stress, drama, chaos, confusion, heartache, grief, and sorrow.

Allow Your peace to rule and reign in my life even in the midst of a chaotic storm. Provide me with the inner peace that I long for so I may make right decisions with a clear mind and peaceful heart.

I ask that Your angels surround me today.

In Jesus' name, Amen!

SCRIPTURE READING

I Peter 5:7 says, "Cast all your anxiety on Him because He cares for you."

Philippians 4:7 says, "And the peace of God, which transcends all understanding, will guard your hearts and your minds in Christ Jesus."

Psalms 29:11 says, "The Lord gives strength to His people; the LORD blesses His people with PEACE."

LET'S PRAY: 30 DAYS OF PRAYER

My Personal Prayer

Shavonda G. McCaleb

Allow Your peace to rule and reign in my life

DAY 10

PRAYER FOR UNSPEAKABLE JOY

Good Morning, Father! This is the day that You have made, and I will rejoice and be glad in it! I am ever so grateful for the love and kindness You continue to show my family and me day after day.

Father, I must be honest with You: on the surface, I appear to be happy, but on the inside, you know better. Today, I ask for Your unspeakable joy that genuinely flows from the inside out. Life has gotten the best of me lately, and I need You to pour into me Your inexpressible joy. The kind of Joy that no matter what I am facing, the joy on the inside will assure me that all will be well.

Father, I don't mind doing the work that it takes for this unspeakable joy. With my hands lifted, I surrender my will to You. I give up anything that may hinder or block me from obtaining Your indescribable joy, the kind of joy that doesn't need to be figured out or explained.

Give me the kind of Joy that allows me to sing and pray at midnight like Paul and Silas. Even when things don't look good from my outside view; what's going on the inside is far greater than what I can see.

Thank You now for pouring Your unspeakable joy into my heart. Thank You for showing me the benefit of staying focused on what's essential, and releasing the things that are draining and taxing to my soul and wellbeing.

In Jesus' name, Amen!

SCRIPTURE READING

Psalms 94:19 says, "When anxiety was great within me, your consolation brought joy to my soul."

James 1:2-3 says, "Consider it pure joy, my brothers and sisters, whenever you face trials of many kinds, because you know that the testing of your faith produces perseverance."

Palms 47:1 says, "Clap your hands, all you nations; shout to God with cries of joy."

My Personal Prayer

Unspeakable joy that genuinely flows from the inside out

DAY 11

PRAYER FOR COURAGE AND BOLDNESS

Today, I come before You like a little lamb that is in need of courage and boldness to speak and stand against wrongdoing. Courage and boldness to do Your will without overthinking my assignment. Courage to stand for right, even when it's unpopular to some and frowned upon by others.

Father, give me the boldness that I need to stand in an upright position against every obstacle and hurdle that is before me. Help me not to become weak and frail when faced with adversity. Lord, stand up in me as I stand up before 'IT.' Give me the confidence in knowing that I am not alone and nothing is impossible for me when You're involved.

Thank You, Father, that I now know and understand through this prayer, you are my helper, and I will not fear what man shall say about or try to do to me *(Hebrews 13:6)*. I have the courage and boldness that I need because You are on my side!

Thank You for the courage and boldness that You have given me today, and as a result, I am more than able to conquer that very thing that I once cried over.

In Jesus' name, Amen!

SCRIPTURE READING

I Chronicles 28:20 says, "David also said to Solomon his son, 'Be strong and courageous, and do the work. Do not be afraid or discouraged, for the LORD God, my God, is with you. He will not fail you or forsake you until all the work for the service of the temple of the LORD is finished.'"

Ephesians 6:10 says, "Finally, be strong in the Lord and in his mighty power."

Psalms 112:7 says, "They will have no fear of bad news; their hearts are steadfast, trusting in the LORD."

LET'S PRAY: 30 DAYS OF PRAYER

My Personal Prayer

Shavonda G. McCaleb

Stand up in me as I stand up before IT

DAY 12

PRAYER FOR UNITY

Father, in the name of Jesus Christ, you are the ultimate peacemaker of all times. I come petitioning You for unity within my family, place of employment, relationship, marriage, this country, in the body of Christ, and between the two of us!

This world we live in can be a cruel and evil place, but even in the midst of turmoil, chaos, and confusion; you are the peacemaker that can speak a word so that peace and unity will reside in that place that once was filled with turmoil.

So, I pray today that You would SPEAK the WORD over my family and bring us closer together and unify us. Speak the word and unite this country. Speak the word and cause unity to begin to form even in the cruelest and most hateful situations. Speak the word Father, and unity will start the healing process of so many broken hearts, spirits and relationships.

I ask that You would order my steps today and give me the wherewithal to bridge some gaps in my own life. Help me to humble myself enough to forgive and forget the wrong that was done to me and the harm I've done to others. Allow me to be that example that You have called me to be so that others may see the light that's inside of me to shine in dark situations.

Use me for Your service. Allow the spirit of unity to be upon me so the lives of Your people I come in contact with will embrace that same sense of unity. Help us to dwell together in UNITY all the days of our lives!

In Jesus' name, Amen!!

SCRIPTURE READING

I Corinthians 1:10 says, "I appeal to you, brothers and sisters, in the name of our Lord Jesus Christ, that all of you agree with one another in what you say and that there be no divisions among you, but that you be perfectly united in mind and thought."

Colossians 3:13-14 says, "Bear with each other and forgive one another if any of you has a grievance against someone. Forgive as the Lord forgave you. And over all these virtues put on love, which binds them all together in perfect unity."

Palms 133:1 says, "How good and pleasant it is when God's people live together in unity!"

LET'S PRAY: 30 DAYS OF PRAYER

My Personal Prayer

SPEAK the WORD over and bring us closer together, and unify us

DAY 13

PRAYER FOR PATIENCE

Father, I need You today and at this very moment! Today, I approach Your throne asking for patience. At times, my life is in constant mayhem because I lack patience. I need You today to cause calmness to enter my life while I wait on You; while I wait on the answers to my pressing questions. Help me to become even-tempered when surrounded by frustrating situations, irritations, and aggravations.

Father, it doesn't take much for me to fly off the handle. I'm tired of being this mean person that I am. I have a good heart, but somewhere along the way, I lost myself. It's embarrassing to continue apologizing for my shortness and inpatient behavior.

Father, I am seeking Your peace and patience in my life. Teach me, and I will learn and apply the lessons that are being taught. I give You my frustration, anger, resentment, and unforgiveness. I'm overwhelmed and feeling burned out with life, so please Father, give me the patience and strength I need to make it through this process. I can't do it with You, I promise You I cannot.

Make me kinder, gentler, more forgiving, softer, and more loving. I pray now for more of Your spirit and less of me. Thank You for hearing my prayer and giving me the strength I need to be patient during this process.

In Jesus' name, Amen!

SCRIPTURE READING

Galatians 5:22 says, "But the fruit of the Spirit is love, joy, peace, patience, kindness, goodness, faithfulness."

Luke 8:15 says, "As for that in the good soil, they are those who, hearing the word, hold it fast in an honest and good heart, and bear fruit with patience."

Ecclesiastes 7:8 says, "Better is the end of a thing than its beginning, and the patient in spirit is better than the proud in spirit."

My Personal Prayer

Make me kinder, gentler, more forgiving, softer, and more loving

DAY 14

PRAYER TO RID INSECURITIES

Heavenly Father, you specialize in calming raging seas and speaking peace in the midst of storms. Thank You for today and what it will bring. Having You in my life assures me of Your power and love You demonstrates day after day.

Father, I need Your help today! I've been too ashamed to say it out loud to others, but You are all knowing, wise, and a loving God. I need help with my insecurities. Somewhere in my life, this seed was planted in my mind to think that I wasn't good enough or I'll never be anything. I must be honest: sometimes my perspective of myself, my life, and even my assignments hinder me from moving forward. I've been dealing with this for years, and I am extremely exhausted.

Father, I'm asking that You help me today. Help me to see myself as You know me. Help me to recognize and appreciate the value that You have placed on the inside of me. Help me to accept and embrace my worth. Help me to love and cherish the beauty with which You have graced me. Help me to see myself through Your eyes. Erase the words that were spoken over my life and set up residence in my mind. Free my mind from those dreams killing words and uproot every seed that was planted.

I not only pray for myself today, but also for others who are struggling with insecurities. Let them know that they are enough, beautiful, valuable, and worthy. I know through prayer that You are too loving and too wise to ever make a mistake. So thank You for being my strength, confidence, and security to conquer my past insecurities.

In Jesus' Name, Amen!

SCRIPTURE READING

Philippians 4:6-9 says, "Do not be anxious about anything, but in every situation, by prayer and petition, with thanksgiving, present your requests to God. And the peace of God, which transcends all understanding, will guard your hearts and your minds in Christ Jesus. Finally, brothers and sisters, whatever is true, whatever is noble, whatever is right, whatever is pure, whatever is lovely, whatever is admirable—if anything is excellent or praiseworthy—think about such things. Whatever you have learned or received or heard from me, or seen in me—put it into practice. And the God of peace will be with you."

LET'S PRAY: 30 DAYS OF PRAYER

My Personal Prayer

Shavonda G. McCaleb

***Help me to see myself as You know me**_

DAY 15

PRAYER TO RELEASE GUILT

Father, I can't keep living like this. I've wronged many people either through my actions or words, and I have been living with this guilt far too long. How much longer do I have to live in this state of sin? I apologized and tried to right my wrongs. I've repented to You, but I am stuck in 'Guilt City.' I feel bad about the decisions I've made in life and my actions that hurt so many.

I know that You are the ultimate forgiver and restorer. I ask again: please forgive me for the wrong that I've done. Create in me a clean heart, so I don't have to continue repeating that unhealthy behavior and living with the guilt of my sins. Father, I open my heart to You completely, with my hands lifted in total surrender. I give You my life all over again!

Please, help me to learn the lesson that is being taught. Help me to learn from my past mistakes so I don't repeat them. Help me to grow past this guilt feeling that is hovering over my head. Help me to realize that beating myself up only delays my progress to move forward. Help me to forgive myself!

Thank You for Your love, grace, mercy and forgiving power. Thank You for restoring me this very moment. Thank You for being a God that allows me to come before you broken, and to leave whole. Thank you for releasing me from the guilt of my past and present.

In Jesus' Name, AMEN!!

SCRIPTURE READING

Isaiah 43:25 says, "I, even I, am the one who blots out your transgression for my own sake, and I'll remember your sins no more."

I John 1:19 says, "God is faithful and reliable. If we confess our sins, he forgives them and cleanses us from everything we've done wrong."

Hebrews 8:12 says, "And I will forgive their wickedness, and I will never again remember their sins."

LET'S PRAY: 30 DAYS OF PRAYER

My Personal Prayer

Shavonda G. McCaleb

Create in me a clean heart

DAY 16

PRAYER TO DANCE TO THE RHYTHM OF GOD

This is the day that You have made, and I am excited about it. This is the day that You have made, and I shall sing Your praises. I have my dancing shoes on, and I can't wait to dance to the Rhythm of Your Heartbeat. This is an excellent day for a dance with You, Father!

Father, today I desire to dance to the rhythm of Your heartbeat! Today my ear is pressed against Your heart. Teach me Your rhythm. Teach me how and when to move. Teach me what and when to speak. Teach me where to go and how long to stay. Allow Your rhythm to spread joy and peace throughout my life and those I come into contact with.

Today, I dance to the rhythm of God. Order my steps in Your word. Teach me to dance after the spirit, so I don't get entangled in the flesh. Help me to stay on beat and not move ahead of You. Teach me how to keep up, so I don't fall behind. Help me not to miss You because of me not paying attention to the beat. Keep me on beat to the lessons You are trying to teach me.

Thank You for allowing me to dance to the rhythm of Your heartbeat. I long to please You and to obey Your word. I long to help win souls for the kingdom. I long to hear You say, "Well done thy good and faithful servant". I long to have another dance with You on tomorrow and forever more.

Thank You again, Father, for allowing me to learn to dance to the rhythm of Your heartbeat.

In Jesus' Name, Amen!

SCRIPTURE READING

2 Samuel 6:14 says, "And David was dancing before the LORD with all his might, and David was wearing a linen ephod."

Psalm 30:11 says, "You have turned for me my mourning into dancing; You have loosed my sackcloth and girded me with gladness…"

Psalm 150:4 says, "Praise Him with timbrel and dancing; Praise Him with stringed instruments and pipe."

My Personal Prayer

Shavonda G. McCaleb

Order my steps in Your word

DAY 17

PRAYER FOR SELF CONTROL

What an incredible privilege it is to come before You on today. Father, I need Your help. I need You to Lead me, Guide me, Walk beside me, Mold me, and Shape me into who You've created me to be. At times, I'm out of jurisdiction with my display of self-control when temptations draw near to me.

Help me, Father, to resist whatever comes my way that is not from You! Help me to be strong and to realize where my help comes from. Help me to think before I speak, even if I am right. Grant me the will-power to remain focused on You and Your Word!

The things that I struggle with today, I lay them at your feet. I surrender them to You. Create in me a clean heart, change my mind, and rid me of the anger, bitterness, pride, jealousy, guilt, and mental processes that continue to bind me.

Father, help me to live a self-controlled life that is led by the Holy Spirit, and the will-power to not give into the things that cause me to become weak and behave out of control. I surrender my thoughts to you; take control of them now.

In Jesus' name, Amen!

SCRIPTURE READING

Galatians 5:16-18 says, "So I say, let the Holy Spirit guide your lives. Then you won't be doing what your sinful nature craves. The sinful nature wants to do evil, which is just the opposite of what the Spirit wants. And the Spirit gives us desires that are the opposite of what the sinful nature desires. These two forces are constantly fighting each other, so you are not free to carry out your good intentions. But when you are directed by the Spirit, you are not under obligation to the law of Moses.

LET'S PRAY: 30 DAYS OF PRAYER

My Personal Prayer

Shavonda G. McCaleb

Help me to be strong and to realize where my help comes from

DAY 18

PRAYER TO ELIMINATE WEAKNESS

Father, I am weak beyond words. My soul, mind, and body are lacking the motivation I need to fight on. I'm weak and need strength to carry on. I am so in need of Your presence and unspeakable joy. I pray that You replace my weakness with Your power, wrapped up in the joy the word talks about. My soul longs for rest. My mind yearns for peace. My body aches for strength.

I know that when I am in Your presence there is the fullness of Joy. I've tried to get into that secret place so I can abide under Your shadow, but I'm too weak to enter in. The cares of life seem to be weighing me down getting the best of me, and I need Your help to eliminate every area of weakness that has overtaken me.

Give me the strength to say 'no' without feeling guilty. Give me the power to stay no when people try to back me into a corner to do things I do not want to do. Stand-up in me so I can stand up to people. I need Your strength to surrender the unhealthy things in my life.

Father, thank You for inclining Your ear to my lips. Thank You for being a God that loves without conditions. Thank You for eliminating the weak areas in my life. And thank You for allowing me to learn from those vulnerable moments in my life. It appears that I am stronger now because of You. I stand boldly in the authority that has been given to me. Thank you for being my Strength in my weak moments.

In Jesus' Name, Amen!

SCRIPTURE READING

2 Corinthians 12:10 says, "Therefore I take pleasure in infirmities, in reproaches, in necessities, in persecutions, in distresses for Christ's sake: for when I am weak, then am I strong."

Daniel 10:18-19 says, "Then this human like figure touched me again and gave me strength. He said, 'Don't be afraid, friend. Peace. Everything is going to be all right. Take courage. Be strong.' Even as he spoke, courage surged up within me. I said, 'Go ahead, and let my master speak. You've given me courage'."

My Personal Prayer

Shavonda G. McCaleb

Eliminate every area of weakness that has overtaken me

DAY 19

PRAYER FOR CLARITY AT A DEAD END

Father, thank You for another opportunity to come before You. I begin with a heavy heart and a minimal vision of seeing my way out of this dead-end situation. The Bible says in Psalms 119:105 that, *"Your word is a lamp to my feet, and a light for my path."* Well, Father, I'm in the dark on a dead-end road, and I have not a clue in which direction to go. If I ever needed You, it's right now!

I pray that the Holy Spirit would lead and guide me from this dark place into the light. My judgment is cloudy with fear, resentment, defeat, and I'm afraid of making the wrong decision. I'm tired of failing over and over again. Father, you said in Your word that if I seek You with my whole heart, I will find You. If I knock, the doors will be opened. And if I ask, it shall be given unto me. Well, I'm asking, seeking and knocking today - I need You now!

Ease the traffic jam on the expressway of my mind. I give You all the anxieties and fears that I am experiencing on the inside of me. I give You the silent frustration that is running rampant through my mind. Speak peace to my soul, and I will be at ease. Without You, I can't move and breathe; I will suffocate if You don't come and see about me. I'm waiting patiently for You, Father. PLEASE provide me the clarity I need concerning where I'm currently standing.

Father, I trust Your word to be true, so I wait patiently for You and Your word to show me the light at the end of this dark and dead-end place. I trust You, so I'll wait for Your road map to get me out of this!

In Jesus' Name, Amen!

SCRIPTURE READING

Psalm 119:130 says, "The unfolding of Your words gives light; It gives understanding to the simple."

Psalm 18:28 says, "For You light my lamp; The LORD my God illumines my darkness."

1 John 1:5 says, "This is the message we have heard from Him and announce to you, that God is Light, and in Him there is no darkness at all."

My Personal Prayer

Shavonda G. McCaleb

Lead and guide me

DAY 20

PRAYER TO TRUST GOD BEYOND THE BROKEN PIECES

Wow, God! I don't know where to start with this prayer because there are so many broken pieces. I have no clue where to begin gathering the fragments of my life. I'm trying to trust You beyond the broken pieces, but every time I think I've arrived at a safe and stable place, something or someone ALWAYS reminds me that I was and still am broken. How do I get passed the broken pieces in my life? If I can't get over them, how can I trust You beyond the brokenness?

Father, I'm trying to do the best I can with the little bit of faith I have left. Help me to trust You 'BEYOND' my broken pieces. I know Your word says that You wouldn't put more on me than I can handle. I heard the word, but it's hard to believe the word from a broken place.

So today, I am going to try it again! I humbly bow in Your presence, and I'm bringing all the many broken and shattered pieces of my life to You, again. I am trusting You to make me whole. I am trusting You to restore me back. I am trusting You to revive me again. I am trusting You to do what You do best, and that's being God and God alone.

I tried piecing things together on my own, only to look at the picture in the end, with remnants and fragments of the broken pieces. BUT GOD, when I place the broken pieces in Your hands, I have the faith to believe that the results will be a breath of fresh air for me to breathe.

So, thank You Father for restoring my faith, trust, and the process of being healed, whole and well in You.

In Jesus' Name, Amen!

SCRIPTURE READING

Jeremiah 17:14-18 says, "God, pick up the pieces. Put me back together again. You are my praise!

Joshua 1:9 says, "Have I not commanded you? Be strong and courageous. Do not be afraid; do not be discouraged, for the LORD your God will be with you wherever you go."

LET'S PRAY: 30 DAYS OF PRAYER

My Personal Prayer

Help me to trust You 'BEYOND' my broken pieces

DAY 21

PRAYER FOR PERSONAL GROWTH

Father, thank You for the privilege of Prayer. I'm thankful today because I serve a God that I can come to at any given moment and just talk. You're not complicated and always readily available to hear the matters of my heart. For that reason alone, I say Thank You!

Father, I noticed that I've been feeling stuck in life. I see others around me up close and personal, and from a distance, growing and making moves. I know that sometimes looks are deceiving, but looking at others has caused me to look at myself, and I realized that I am at a standstill in life.

Year after year, I find myself in the same place and doing the same things. I want to GROW! I no longer want to be stuck and not producing fruit. Help me today to be the best person I was created to be. Restore the passion that I once had so that I can build and grow from the current place in which I stand.

Father, give me a strategic plan for my personal growth. Plant me in the right fertile soil so I can grow. Connect me with likeminded people who will come along and water the seed that is within me. And allow Your Son, Jesus Christ, to shine on me so I may get the nutrients I need to sprout up and start producing good fruit.

Father, thank You! I trust the process, and I look forward to my personal growth in You first. I surrender my will to You, and I am willing, without hesitation to do the work. Speak to me; I am listening to the plans You have for my personal growth.

In Jesus' Name, Amen!

SCRIPTURE READING

1 John 3:2 says, "Beloved, we are God's children now, and what we will be has not yet appeared; but we know that when he appears we shall be like him, because we shall see him as he is."

Galatians 1:12 says, "For I did not receive it from any man, nor was I taught it, but I received it through a revelation of Jesus Christ."

2 Peter 3:18 says, "But grow in the grace and knowledge of our Lord and Savior Jesus Christ. To him be the glory both now and to the day of eternity. Amen."

LET'S PRAY: 30 DAYS OF PRAYER

My Personal Prayer

Shavonda G. McCaleb

Help me today to be the best person I was created to be

DAY 22

PRAYER TO DISCHARGE DEPRESSION

Father, thank You for allowing me to come before you again. I value the time we spend together. I believe that the prayers I've prayed up until this point have made me better and not bitter, and I am forever learning by spending time with you that there is always room for growth and improvement.

So, here I am again, Father asking You to help me discharge depression from my life. I know that believers don't deal with it head on, they blame it on the devil. Well, I am not doing that today. Depression is real, and it first starts with admission. I admit that I battle (secretly) with depression. I battle secretly because I am ashamed of what others may think of me. You see, they are only looking from the outside in, but if they would actually open the door, come in and take a seat, they would realize that I've been depressed for years right in plain sight.

Father, I want to be free from depression. I want to operate in the fullness of You, Your love, joy, and peace. I need You to discharge depression from my mind, thought process, perspective on life, and every area that it has set up residence. Cast it out of my mind. DISMISS it now in the name of Jesus!

I realize that now that you have dismissed it, there is now an empty space. FILL IT UP with Your pureness, holiness, love, peace, joy, humility, tenderness, laughter, and more of You! I decree and declare today that I am whole and well in You. I decree and declare that my mind is right in You. I decree and declare that depression is no longer welcomed to visit, sleepover, camp out, live, or occupy any areas of my life. I take authority of my mind through You and the word.

In Jesus' Name, Amen!

SCRIPTURE READING

Psalm 34:17-18 says, "When the righteous cry for help, the Lord hears and delivers them out of all their troubles. The Lord is near to the brokenhearted and saves the crushed in spirit."

Matthew 11:28 says, "Come to me, all who labor and are heavy laden, and I will give you rest."

1 Peter 5:7 says, "Casting all your anxieties on him, because he cares for you."

My Personal Prayer

Shavonda G. McCaleb

Discharge depression from my life

DAY 23

PRAYER FOR PERSEVERANCE - HOW MUCH LONGER?

Father, I bless and thank You for a brand-new day wrapped up in new mercies, opportunities, and challenges that this day may bring. I pray as I walk throughout this day that You would go with me. Keep me focused and in tuned to what the Spirit is saying. Help me not to give up and give in to the things that are designed to cause me to stumble and fall.

Looking at my life, I realize that the struggle has been long, hard and it's real. How much longer do I have to fight, struggle, and play tug of war with this thing called life?

Help me to persevere through the hurdles and roadblocks of this day. Help me not to become weary and lose my focus. Help me not to forget because of the things I am too afraid to face. Help me to push through it – pass it.

Father, help me to remain steadfast, unmovable always abounding in Your work. With You on my side, I know that I Can and I Will Persevere. I will not give up. I will continue to press forward, trusting and believing Your Word!

So, Father, thank You for this time we've shared together. Thank You for giving me the strength and confidence that I needed today to Persevere. I have the tenacity and strength to keep on keeping on!

In Jesus' Name, Amen!

SCRIPTURE READING

I Corinthians 15:58 says, "Therefore, my beloved brethren, be ye steadfast, unmovable, always abounding in the work of the Lord, for ye know that your labor is not in vain in the Lord."

James 1:12 says, "Blessed is the man who remains steadfast under trial, for when he has stood the test he will receive the crown of life, which God has promised to those who love him."

Galatians 6:9 says, "And let us not grow weary of doing good, for in due season we will reap, if we do not give up."

My Personal Prayer

Shavonda G. McCaleb

Help me to persevere through the hurdles and roadblocks

DAY 24

PRAYER OF EXALTATION

Father, Your name is above all names. You're worthy of all my praise. Mighty are the works of Your hands. You are an excellent God, one who sits high and looks low. The one who knows us from the inside out. Thank You for being a present help at the time of trouble. Thank You for loving me when I didn't extend that same love back to You. Thank You for your continual grace and mercy that's spread to me day after day.

You are a wise and loving God. You've covered me even in my naked moments in life. You've kept me even when I didn't want to be kept. I lift Your name on high because You are worthy to be praised and worshipped. I glorify You for being a present help in the time of trouble. I adore You because without You I am nothing. I give You glory because You are the Great I AM!

With my whole heart, mind, body, and soul, I praise You, Lord! You are omnipresent, everywhere at the same time. You are omniscient: you know all things. You are my zenith, the highpoint of my life. I exalt You today Father because You are not an absent Father, you are forever present, and I give You Glory for being here.

Thank You for being the God of Abraham, Isaac, and Jacob – but more importantly, THANK YOU for being my God!

Hallelujah, Hallelujah, Hallelujah and Amen!

SCRIPTURE READING

Psalms 69:30 says, "I will praise God's name with song and exalt Him with thanksgiving."

Psalms 71:23 says, "My lips shall exult when I sing psalms unto thee; and my soul, which thou hast redeemed."

Psalms 99:9 says, "Exalt the LORD our God, and worship at his holy hill; for the LORD our God is holy."

LET'S PRAY: 30 DAYS OF PRAYER

My Personal Prayer

Shavonda G. McCaleb

Thank You for being a present help at the time of trouble

DAY 25

PRAYER OF NEWNESS

Father God, thank You for all things. I come to You today for a portion of newness. My old ways of doing things seem to be overshadowing my life, and I am suffocating. I need something new and fresh in my life, something that will provide fuel to my diming fire.

Breathe on me the breath of life. I make room in my mind, heart, body, and soul for You to dwell. Father, I pray, through this prayer that anything in my life that is not like You that You would get rid of the old that is taking up unnecessary space and replace it with the new things You've desired for me to have. A new mind, unique perspective, new attitude, new way of thinking, a new heart, new conversations, and a new walk-in You.

Thank you, Father! Even in this prayer, I feel Your fresh air blowing from a different direction. I'm feeling the newness of life, and I thank You for it right now, in the name of Jesus!

Thank You for this wonderful time we've spent together. I am convinced that the newness I'm feeling right now is wrapped up in Your Love, and I Thank You for it!

In Jesus' Name, Amen!

SCRIPTURE READING

1 Peter 1:3 says, "Blessed be the God and Father of our Lord Jesus Christ, who according to His great mercy has caused us to be born again to a living hope through the resurrection of Jesus Christ from the dead…"

2 Peter 3:1 says, "But according to His promise we are looking for new heavens and a new earth, in which righteousness dwells."

2 Corinthians 5:17 says, "Therefore if any man be in Christ, he is a new creature: old things are passed away; behold, all things are become new."

My Personal Prayer

Shavonda G. McCaleb

Breathe on me the breath of life

DAY 26

PRAYER FOR KNOWING JESUS MORE

Father, thank You for Your Word. It is a lamp to my feet and it lights my path. Thank You that even during dark and difficult times, you are that light that sits on the hill that cannot and will not be hidden. Thank You for being my compass and roadmap in this life. At times, I may not follow the path You have set out for me, and I end up on dark and windy roads with no sense of direction. Help me to stay on track. Help me not to take unnecessary stops and turns along the way.

I desire to please You with the life I live. I wish to walk after the spirit and not fulfill the lust of the flesh. I want to know You better, more and more each day. Father, I see this journey that I am on was strategically planned out just for me. My prayer today is that I will know more about You. More of your love, more of your compassion, more of Your unselfishness, more of Your ministry, and more of your suffering. I pray for more of You!

Father, I understand that this request requires my participation and I am willing to do the work it requires to bring me closer to You and know You more. Thank You for accepting me as I am. Thank You for being willing to allow me into Your personal space so that I can learn more about You more deeply and spiritually. Thank You for being my teacher and letting me be the student. I am ready to learn more about You.

In Jesus' Name, Amen!

SCRIPTURE READING

2 Peter 3:18 says, "but grow in the grace and knowledge of our Lord and Savior Jesus Christ To Him be the glory, both now and to the day of eternity. Amen.

1 John 2:3 says, "By this we know that we have come to know Him, if we keep His commandments."

John 10:14 says, ""I am the good shepherd, and I know My own and My own know Me…"

LET'S PRAY: 30 DAYS OF PRAYER

My Personal Prayer

Shavonda G. McCaleb

I wish to walk after the spirit and not fulfill the lust of the flesh

DAY 27

PRAYER OF LEARNING - SCHOOL IS IN SESSION

Father, thank You for the privilege of prayer and another opportunity to come before You with a humbled heart. Father, today I begin with an opened heart and mind to learn of Your ways. I was told that when the student is READY, the teacher will SHOW up. Well, Father, I'm not only ready, but I am willing with no reluctance to receive the lessons that You are about to teach me.

Father, teach me how to pray, teach me how to be generous, teach me how to forgive, teach me how to wait in Your presence, teach me how to lead by example, show me how to walk according to Your Word, teach me how to do Your Will. Teach me Your Word. Father, I stretch my hands to You, the all-knowing God, believing that You are the most excellent teacher of all. I want to learn Your ways. I desire to sit at Your feet ready to learn from You.

My heart, mind, and soul are ready, willing and able to embrace Your truths. Teach me, and I will be taught. Teach me, and I will be able to show others. Teach me, and I will be the epitome of a true disciple of Jesus Christ. I surrender my will, perspective and thought process to You. I fully empty out myself so You can fill me up with Your righteousness.

Thank You in advance for the lessons that I am about to learn from You. With my hands lifted up, I surrender my will to Yours!

In Jesus Name, Amen!

SCRIPTURE READING

Proverbs 1:7 says, "The fear of the LORD is the beginning of knowledge, but fools despise wisdom and instruction."

Proverbs 2:6 says, "For the LORD gives wisdom; from his mouth come knowledge and understanding."

Proverbs 18:15 says, "The heart of the discerning acquires knowledge, for the ears of the wise seek it out."

My Personal Prayer

Shavonda G. McCaleb

Father, teach me

DAY 28

PRAYER FOR THE CHASE - DON'T GET TIRED

Father, I woke up this morning with thanksgiving in my heart, clapping in my hands, and running in my feet. I'm chasing after You today. I know that I have allowed the cares of this world to dictate my relationship with You, and for that, I repent!

I know that at times I've chased after money, fame, material things, relationships, people, places and things; all of which have left me with an empty void. But I know this: chasing after You adds value to my life. Help me to stay on track this time. Help me not to become wearing during the chase. Help me not to lose consciousness. Help me to stay awake and not get tired during the quest.

When my flesh is weak, wake up my spiritual man to take over the chase. I know that I can do all things in Your son Jesus Christ, who gives me strength.

I thank You for giving me the power I need to continue the chase. I thank You that I am no longer weary, but I am adequately equipped with the necessary tools I need to run on and see what the end is going to be.

In Jesus' Name, Amen!

SCRIPTURE READING

Matthew 6:33 says, "But seek first his kingdom and his righteousness, and all these things will be given to you as well."

Deuteronomy 4:29 says, "But if from there you seek the Lord your God, you will find him if you seek him with all your heart and with all your soul."

Psalms 63:1 says, "You, God, are my God, earnestly I seek you; I thirst for you, my whole being longs for you, in a dry and parched land where there is no water"

My Personal Prayer

Shavonda G. McCaleb

Help me to stay awake and not get tired

DAY 29

PRAYER FOR A DRINK
(LET'S HAVE A DRINK OF THE LIVING WATER)

Father, thank You for allowing me to be in my right mind; the kind of mind that leads me besides the still waters. The kind of mind that shows me the paths I need to take to find the living water to quench my thirsty soul. Father, thank You for being my thirst quencher.

In you Father, I know that you have exactly what I need to draw from Your well. The Well of Living Water. My soul is thirsty for You. I tried drinking from other people, places, and things, only to find myself needing another drink! I'm tired of drawing again and again and again, a daunting repeat of drawing and never being fulfilled.

Dismantle this cycle in my life. Lead me to the well of living water so my soul will never thirst again. Give me a drink of the living water my soul longs for, and my thirst can finally be quenched.

Father, my soul is thirsting for You and Your righteousness. With my handles lifted up, and my mouth filled with praise, and a heart of thanksgiving, I bless You O Lord.

Thank you for being my thirst quencher. Thank you that I no longer have to seek or search for imitation drinks because I have now found a well that never runs dry, a well filled with living water. Thank You, Father, for the best drink I've ever had in my life.

In Jesus' name, Amen!

SCRIPTURE READING

John 4:14 says, "But whoever drinks of the water that I will give him shall never thirst; but the water that I will give him will become in him a well of water springing up to eternal life."

John 7:38 says, "He who believes in Me, as the Scripture said, 'From his innermost being will flow rivers of living water."

Psalms 42:1-2 says, "As the deer pants for the water, so my soul pants for You, O God. My soul thirsts for God, for the living God; When shall I come and appear before God?"

LET'S PRAY: 30 DAYS OF PRAYER

My Personal Prayer

Shavonda G. McCaleb

Lead me to the well of living water

DAY 30

PRAYER OF BREAKING NEWS

Father, Thank You! As I close out this 30 days of prayer, I want You to know that I have enjoyed sitting at Your feet, resting in Your arms, and just spending time with You. I thank You for the corrections, directions, and modifications You have made throughout my life for the past 30 days. Sometimes I became distracted and lost hope, but I realized something – You've never abandoned me on this journey called life.

I thank You, Father, for the Breaking News of today: *"The good news is that the bad news was wrong."* Everything the enemy tried to convince me of was nothing more than a plot and plan to keep me stuck. O God, I thank You for backing up Your spiritual tow truck to my life and pulling me up and out! I thank You Father because when I didn't have the strength to carry on, you lifted me up. I now have the spiritual tenacity to carry on.

I am better today because of You. I am whole and well in You. I am no longer in pieces, but I am walking, and living in peace. I thank You because I am no longer suffocating, but I am breathing again, and it feels good! I thank You because I've searched all over trying to find a thirst quencher. I've experienced some unmentionable places to draw from, but the living water that You've provided me has left me satisfied and well pleased.

Father, thank You for the Breaking News of the day: *"The good news is that the bad news was wrong."* I WIN!

In Jesus' Name, Amen!

SCRIPTURE READING

Proverbs 25:25 says, "Like cold water to a weary soul, so is good news from a distant land."

Proverbs 15:30 says, "Bright eyes gladden the heart; Good news puts fat on the bones."

Luke 2:10 says, "But the angel said to them, "Do not be afraid. I bring you good news of great joy that will be for all the people."

LET'S PRAY: 30 DAYS OF PRAYER

My Personal Prayer

Shavonda G. McCaleb

"The good news is that the bad news was wrong."

WE BELIEVE

WOW, how powerful were those last 30 days in the presence of God? I'm sure you have experienced a rollercoaster of emotions: tears, joys, liberation, salvation, repentance, and a sense of freedom just to name a few. Allow me to encourage you to continue to seek the face of God and wrap everything that concerns you in prayer. By doing so, you will discover that the hands of God are more prominent and remarkably stronger to carry the matters of your heart. Even when it doesn't seem like anything is working in your favor, trust the process in the hands you've placed your concerns in.

What do I do now? You continue your prayer journey believing that everything concerning you will work out for your good. You continue to believe that even though it doesn't feel right, everything is working for your good. You continue to believe that it may hurt, sting, or burn for now, but everything is working for your good. Just like a diamond in the ruff, before you could see the real beauty of it, what happens beneath the surface is what makes a diamond, a diamond!

You see, the journey of a diamond is extremely long and a complicated process. The word 'Diamond' comes from the Greek word, "Adamas" and means "unconquerable and indestructible." Before they are displayed for everyone to admire and eventually love, they are beneath the earth covered in dirt and rooted in darkness. After a diamond is recovered, it has to go through a 'process' of mining, sorting, and cutting. It is considered the hardest natural substance found on Earth. Now, how much different are you compared to a diamond?

In life, we will experience a multiplicity of challenges but always remember your perspective on a situation has everything to do with your response to the outcome. Never forget, you are 'STRONG,' 'UNCONQUERABLE,' AND 'INDESTRUCTIBLE'! Continue to keep your ear pressed to God's lips, and He will speak.

Hey, Let's Pray!

-Shavonda McCaleb

ABOUT THE AUTHOR

Shavonda G. McCaleb was born with a purpose, power, passion, and a vision for storytelling. Shavonda's writing inspires, empowers, encourages, and transcends throughout a multiplicity of lives and communities. She considers herself "merely a pencil in God's hand, and He is doing the writing." Shavonda walks on purpose, talks on purpose, and breathes on purpose. Her spiritual journey impacts, infect and empowers.

Shavonda is the Founder and Chief Executive Officer of Positively Impacting Communities (PIC) Foundation Inc. She is the proud mother of two children, Jonathan and Camry (her daughter Camry is deaf). Shavonda understood from personal experience with Camry's hearing loss that more needed to be done within the deaf and hard of hearing community. As a result, she founded the PIC Foundation to be that advocate and resource for the deaf and hard of hearing communities.

Shavonda strives to positively impact the lives of those who she comes in contact with, through her inspirational messages, words of encouragement, speaking/teaching, writings and her personal life. Shavonda is the author of five books, and she is currently working on her sixth book. She also writes for BOLD Favor Magazine (Atlanta, GA).

Shavonda served as one of the Board of Directors of Georgia Center for the Deaf and Hard of Hearing (formerly GACHI). She is also part of the National Association of Professional Women (NAPW), and a Certified Professional Life Coach (American Association of Christian Counselors - AACC)

Shavonda's dreams, aspirations, and goals are to "positively impact" the lives of people and the communities which she encounters, starting with one person at a time. Her passion for the deaf and hard of hearing community reaches beyond herself and is a beautiful reflection of a Life of Servanthood.

www.ingramcontent.com/pod-product-compliance
Lightning Source LLC
Chambersburg PA
CBHW031646040426
42453CB00006B/222